M000098777

PIECES

Poetry & Prose

By

Ejspeaks

WITH A FOREWORD BY

ERICA FOREMAN

Copyright 2017 Ejspeaks ⓔⓙ

No part of this book may be used, duplicated or performed without written consent of the author.

All rights reserved

ISBN-13: 978-0998994000

ISBN-10: 0998994006

www.ejspeaks.com

To Fredrick, Raylen & Braxton and perhaps those to come.
You are everything to me.

Table of Contents

Breath

Loosed

FOREWORD

When Evette told me she was writing a book, I thought 'It's about darn time!'. I knew she had it in her to give us a raw and untainted view of her world, but never did I think she would give us the keys to her heart and passion. As she let me read the PIECES of her work as she completed them, I increasingly became in awe. Not just by the poems themselves, but by the emotions and story behind the words in plain sight. This was different side of the EJ that I knew. I knew her as my creative partner, my comedic twin. We both perform spoken word, but this was leaps and bounds beyond what I imagined this book would be.

As a creative mind and writer, myself, I am always interested to see how people unfold their truths and tell their stories. How they capture the world and share it with others. Will they only frame the best pictures they were able to capture? Will they tear down the walls and let you into their reality? Am I inspired or changed after you distributed your art?

A year ago, this time, I came across Ejspeaks on Facebook, her video kept coming up on my timeline so I finally decided to watch one. The first video I ever watched was "When Grandmothers Finally Call To Pick Up Your Kids". Can I tell you I laughed so hard and out of nowhere, I confused a client at work (totally out of order and I do not condone watching Youtube or social media videos at work). That video went into "Arguing with the Bill Collector" to the "You Are Not Fat Video" to countless others until I was caught up on all videos on all social media platforms. By this time, Ejspeaks was my "friend" in my head. You know how you may watch Taraji P. Henson or anyone you connect to on television and make a relationship up "in your head"? Yep, that was me.

At this time in life, I had started my journey pursuing my dream to produce great content for television and film, meanwhile, another young lady several states away from me, was following her calling towards becoming a comedic personality and writer. I knew that we were two creative minds that if ever met, could change the world together. Through God's divine intervention, I leapt out on faith and reached out to her on social media, got nothing- Just like black folks☺ I found an email address at the end of one of her videos on YouTube one day, by chance, and reached out. Long story short, I flew out to meet her and her team for business and the rest was history. Regardless of how funny this talented woman is, she is like an octagon, as soon as you get to know one side of her she has another side that is just as intriguing and makes you want to know the full story behind her jokes and poetry.

I have learned over the course of this year that Evette has learned and mastered the art of taking life as she has been given it, mix it with her passion and gifts, and create some of the most truthful, hilarious, thought-provoking work I have ever come across. To consider the extreme challenges she has had to endure and joys she has proudly accepted to create this piece of work blesses me. From every phone call to every email, from every tear to every laugh, this was a journey I will always remember. I am utterly proud of you and your accomplishment in this book. Not just because of its completion, but also because of the growth I have witnessed in the process. This is simply the beginning of the great things God has destined for you. Whether you're getting to it or getting through it, the movement is the same so keep crawling, keep walking, keep running…don't stop until you arrive. ~Unknown

To the readers: I pray that as you read each word, embrace each line, turn each page; you grow, you are inspired, you release, you gain, you tear down, you build up, and most importantly…you love and LIVE.

"I believe that if life gives you lemons, you should make lemonade…And then try to find somebody whose life has given them vodka, and have a party" Ron White

You are my vodka. LOL.

#Cheers

INTRODUCTION

This collection represents *pieces* of pain and triumph, growth and brokenness. Some are *pieces* of my past, others aren't even my *pieces*. I have been so overwhelmingly blessed to witness life, first and second hand, by breasted warriors and survivors who were humbly rooted in the Earth, determined not to die. They were bold enough to be humanly transparent. I saw them break into *pieces* during the storm, and I saw them use those same *pieces* to build strength. These truths are relentless, they are real, and they are the *pieces* that built me. And because they weren't afraid nor ashamed to live, sometimes with just *pieces*, I am whole. These *pieces* made me.

ROOT

I.

A BIT DIFFERENT

The womenfolk.

The Aunts.

They were waiting on my velvet to snap, my walk to change-
my hips to burst, my smell to permeate.

They figured the summer heat would bring out the lions

that would prey on my virgin flesh, and would win.

He had been lurking for quite some time.

They waited on my thighs to spread, my teeth to grow.

They watched me from their kitchen conferences

to see if my eyes could decode the language of women.

They waited behind doors, whispering, to see my voice spread;

to see if my chest widened my when I spoke.

Now, only one foot hit the floor when I sat,

while the other conversed with the wind.

I toiled with my hair six times a day.

And I loved for my skin to smell like lavender.

It was autumn when the lion gently broke me.

And the Aunts were well aware.

JEWELS

I drowned my uterus in alkaline.

Ate of the ground, fed Earth to the world.

Massaged my womb with scriptures

to prepare for the arrival.

Life growing inside of me.

Me, a walking habitation- a brown ecosystem,

became full and ready

my water broke and Holy oil seeped down my leg.

Cracked the bone in my hip

opened up this goldmine and gave birth to black diamonds.

Held my most prized possessions,

and spoke life before the world could loose death.

"Children, always shine.

In a world, where they will question your crystals,

try to name them stone, Shine!

Try to fool you, dress you in zirconium.

Try to shatter you, but you are not cheap glass!

Children, even in the dark places, shine!

And know that you are exquisite. Perfectly cut.

You are a black diamond,

don't answer to anything else."

BUTTERFLY BABY

My father never expected me to grow,
just assumed I'd wilt in his absence, in a stale caucus of a caterpillar.
I can only imagine his offense
to seeing my wings,
though he never taught me how to fly.

DAYCARE

She thought she could make a man of him.

But by the time the he came,

and the baby did too,

she realized the three of them, were all children.

PETALS

He loves me.

He loves me not.

He loves me.

He loves me not.

While others pluck, and gamble on the existence of a dying petal,

I am arguing with truths.

How frail of me to hang in the balance of flower,

who, even in death is more developed than my legs

that have yet to walk away from an indecisive heart.

Signals are mixed, and when they are clear,

I distort them for second chances.

He loves me.

He loves me not.

He loves me.

He loves me not.

BROKEN HERO

She was the third baby to stretch my skin,
turned my stomach into chewing gum.
I lost control of my hormones,
couldn't stop spitting or sucking on penny candy.
She disfigured my body. Changed my life forever.
And I have failed her so many times.
Sometimes around midnight, when her lids are tightly closed,
and her mind is busy dreaming,
I pray she forgives me for each time I left my cape.
For each time my humanly flesh interfered with my super powers.
I only wanted to be her hero.
I wish I could watch her from the school gate at recess, give her a script
for bullies and mean girls.
Prepare her for cold winters, equip her for wars within.
I wish I could go back to that day in November,
when I saw the evil proof on her innocent thighs.
Dammit, I left my cape.
Where the hell is my cape!
I could see my reflection in his fluids, while they lay on her tainted skin.
I froze in fear, in pain.
I am still thawing out.
So I hid her- tried to heal her; built a house of steel around her.
No one enters. No one leaves. No one ever gets hurt again.
We just miss out on living.
Miss out on the sun.
Miss out on the rainbows and sleepovers
And everything else that seems normal.
We both were too young to understand how any of this works,
And I pray someday, we both forgive me.

FAMILIAR

I have always hated trying new things.
I suppose that's why I'm still with you.

IRONY

How ironic, on the fourth trip from the abortion clinic-
receipt on the dash, purse on the floorboard, arms folded,
tattooed against my chest.
I am angry because he doesn't ask me how I feel.
The nerve of me to want love,
although I will do nothing but suck it back out.
How ironic for him to have 4 cars, but no drive.
Never going anywhere, always cumming,
though I never showed the proof.
How ironic, making plans to enjoy life,
all while being a walking cemetery.
Tombstones embedded in my uterus,
and ghosts inhabiting my fallopian tubes.
I have the nerve to be afraid of haunted houses, when I am Halloween.
How ironic to get abortions
because they are cheaper than raising children,
but condoms are a dollar, and common sense is just too expensive.
Isn't it ironic,
that it just wasn't a good time to have a baby?
My peace of mind was more important,
but every night around the third watch,
I hear vacuums and whispers, mimicking tiny breaths.
And by morning I only have a piece of my mind.
The rest is occupied by first trimester fetal cries-

sound like nails digging in my ears,

sound like hell, awaiting my arrival,

sound like the devil, telling me thank you.

I felt a tear drop from God's face, and wondered why He still cared.

Isn't it ironic,

that I am non-violent, non-confrontational?

I would never hurt a soul- unless it was growing in the pit of my belly.

And isn't it ironic, that I love to dress pretty,

but all I wear is conviction and guilt.

And it is an itchy sweater,

draped over a rebellious and voluntary barren womb

that refuses to deal with life.

It is uncomfortable, and heavy, and obvious and defecating

and it is hot and it is present

and although I never physically put it on,

ironically I wear it every single day.

MIRROR TALK
(WHEN I'M FEELING FANCY)

"You are the bomb, girl!

Look at you, looking all explosive and stuff!!

Dontchu hurt nobody.

Look at your hips, rocking and swaying

causing all types of hazards and thangs.

Look at your thighs, swollen and full,

stealing all types of attention and thangs.

Look at your lips, your face. Check out your aura!

Girl you something else!

Be careful with yo' fine self today!"

SHORE BOUND

I never learned how to swim.
My mother never learned.
My grandmother never learned.
My great grandmother never learned.
I am afraid to go under it.
They keep telling us to get over it.
But we've discovered that the safest waters
are those contained by porcelain.

CROWDED QUEEN

I consumed her, for him.

Changed my preference, personified queer.

Aligned our nipples to quench his hunger for more.

Stacked our pelvises, wet cave to wet cave

for his body to vomit.

Mathematical mattress, adding bodies, subtracting my space;

Thought it could divide him, give us each an equal share.

though I'm not sure why...She was only a guest, not a tenant.

The bed, still doing math, adding juices

multiplied by clits, subtracting my standards,

I am almost down to zero, tucked my remainder under the fitted sheet

so I could have some for myself when this is over.

When is this gonna be over?

I have morphed into her. Her sweat is now my sweat,

though we all glisten from the heat of a burning marriage.

She is stuffing herself down my throat,

he is stuffing himself inside of me.

I wonder, are they trying to meet in my stomach?

We are now an exhibit of bodies, turning, shifting, sliding, swapping.

He loves this moment. She loves this moment,

And I left before it got started,

though they are still gnawing on my flesh.

They are hungry for this broken buffet,

while I starve for a spot in my own bed.

When is this gonna be over?

NUMBER BLUE

He is the very air I breathe,
No wonder I am suffocating.

SOUTHERN

Quiet conversations tip toe on the kitchen table.

Secret recipes bind the family, and hot meals greet the menfolk.

We trade stories about our days on the front porch

while we wave at passersby.

The mosquitos eventually win, and the crickets take the choir stand.

And all that is left is big mama's flyswatter.

We learn to dance with generational curses.

Become comfortable, not moving.

Rugs are as tall as the sunflower crop;

How else will we conceal the infidelities and outside children?

And uncles with busy hands?

Curtains hide sibling rivalries and the complexities of colorism.

And though we argue loud, the aging floors are much louder.

Air conditioners stick out windows,

but the girls approaching puberty stick out more.

I pray they are careful.

The house plays hotel to every related squatter,

and the longest dirt road is still cleaner than the box of family secrets.

The poverty line is drawn with railroad tracks,

and I have never been ashamed of my side of town.

Church fans and bibles, music and repentance.

Some struggle to leave this place we call home,

while others escape as soon as they can.

We are not perfect, until The Sabbath.

And what's a Sunday, without Soul Food?

17

DEPENDENT

I miss you.

The constant presence of another.

Body heat on my bed.

Your scent in my car.

Unafraid of creaky floors, and squeaky doors,

because you were there.

I miss picking up after you;

seeing your boots tucked away in the corner

reassuring me that you had not left.

I miss the conversation.

The shared utility bill.

And help bringing in the groceries.

It's been two weeks and I hate being alone…

so I bought some new lipstick, cut my split ends

and bought a new welcome mat.

I should have your replacement by tomorrow.

NUMBER YELLOW

Some days, I like to trick him

Put on a fancy dress

Classy shoes

Huge smile

Make him think I've moved on.

I be lying.

BONE
II.

CARRY

Those that formed waters inside of me,

Broke waters to get out of me,

Cause me to shed the most waters of them all.

FLAWS

My teeth, the way they turn.

The thickened skin on my calloused feet.

My stretched skin that resembles the art of a toddler.

My face, painted in moles.

My broken uterus, the way it sinks inside of me.

My credit.

My attitude, every 21 days.

My heart, the way it still loves those who reject me.

UNCLE MARVIN

Uncle Marvin had shiny lips, smooth cuticles, clean pores.

He was "that" kind of man.

He came around and folk whispered, folk nudged their elbows,

judged with their eyes. Uncle Marvin glided anyhow.

At times, the insults would roll off his blazers or bounce off his trousers.

He was just that resilient. Mystical even.

Had a best friend, like any other girl. He and Joe were giddy.

Knew all the tea, sipped all the tea, were tickled by said tea and

unbothered by the commoners.

Unmoved by the folk who lived in cages of restriction.

As children, we gazed in amazement as Uncle Marvin crossed his legs.

Never seen slacks twist so smooth.

Like his foot actually belonged in midair.

His two fingers had an intimate affair with Newport longs.

His smoke danced a hypnotic curving in big mama's living room.

It clouded her television,

covered some random white lady trying to win some money on jeopardy

And we were in awe.

We were enticed, couldn't have cared less about the second hand smoke.

He even steered his car with one hand so he wouldn't miss a puff.

watched the children and taught the women a few things.

He was brown silk. He was necessary.

He spoke liquid gold,

not one second did he ever think that he didn't know everything.

We didn't realize it then,

but we would soon yearn for this type of confidence in a world that cuts
so deep.

We would soon need his walk undeterred, no matter the voices around.

Would soon need his consistency no matter the angle in which the
world turns or tilts.

Uncle Marvin died of renal failure- I assume from all the tea.

Though the townsfolk said, it was because he was "that" type of man.

That's what they always say about "those" type of men.

The fairies. The gays. The sissies.

Though I don't think Uncle Marvin would have cared.

He never did.

SHOES

I went and bought some new shoes today.

I promised myself I wouldn't scuff them, begging a man to stay.

I always tear my shoes, when love leaves early.

It's almost like me and love are keeping time on two different clocks

and right when I think love is just getting started,

that's when love clocks out.

I don't know, maybe it's me.

Maybe love can't tell time.

Maybe the batteries in the clock don't even work.

Maybe love ain't even love, just something I keep calling it

because I don't want to deal with the fact that

I keep falling for something without a name.

Either way, this time, I'm not scuffing up my new shoes.

TIS ANOTHER DAY

I've never met him in the flesh.

Personify him with the sunshine.

Grateful for his return in the undeniable rays.

Speaks to me softly, though I can't pinpoint the tone.

I can only hear a feeling.

Know he's there by my lack of anxiety.

Lack of meltdowns. Lack of fear.

Sometimes I meet him on my knees, converse about my day.

Sometimes,

we meet in my secret place and I just simply wave my hands.

Feel him betwixt my fingers;

wade through the circumstances of thick life.

He is thicker. Thank you God for being thicker.

He is the loudest quiet.

Rocks my children to sleep, when my songs are out of key.

Puts my home at peace, when I am the one who started the war.

He moves, so that I am still.

I obey, even in confusion.

I've never met him in the flesh

Personify him with each new day,

Thank you God, for meeting me again.

WASHING THE MEN AWAY

Where are the waters that wash the men away?

The waters that cleanse from residues left by all the John Does?

I thought he had a name.

None of them have names.

Only identified by the smell they left once they put their clothes back on.

I stink, smell like several.

I smell like many.

Smell like legions.

Need to baptize my fruit in blessed oil.

Purge out the handprints.

Douche out the specimens.

He went in my canal and pulled out a chunk of more men;

they must have been hiding.

Where are the waters that can flush out the bodily stains,

shed this layer of used up, rinse off their flesh?

Because this bath

nor these dry prayers

nor the scrubbing

is working.

VAIN STRENGTH

I am the strongest I have ever been.

I am unbreakable. I am steel. I am still. Unshakable.

Needing nothing of anyone.

My bones don't bend, and my muscles don't move.

I promised pain, that it would never win again.

So I got strong.

And now I am so strong,

that I am nothing else.

Not happy

Not loving

Not bubbly

Not fulfilled

Not comforted

Just

Strong.

Strong for no reason at all.

HUNGRY AMERICA

We must taste like gold,

maybe that's we are being swallowed up by white soil?

Maybe our flesh taste like heaven?

How can the ground ever satisfy its hunger

when it has no stomach- just a craving for brown bodies?

I wonder,

do they ever take the time to hear the wailings of the black women?

Anguish in the key of agony, from burying their children.

The graveyard, a lower level playground

full of naked bones, freshly shed of melanin

while shredded sheets of The Willie Lynch Letter are bound in the dirt.

I wonder

do they notice that the dirt has now turned to mud from the weepings

of the children who have lost their fathers?

No wonder our feet sink with each step.

We are left with memories of men.

We only remember being protected,

can only reminisce on being covered.

I wonder

do they ever hear the breath leave our brown bodies,

or do they carelessly mistake it for a summer breeze?

Inhaling and exhaling from black lungs is so expensive.

Yet with no currency, it is a price we continue to pay-

black body bartering.

I wonder will they ever admit, that they are still addicted to strange fruit.

Not satisfied until we are plucked from among them.

Still addicted to the smell of decayed black flesh,

just to get the day started.

Still addicted to the oppressed attempting to rise.

They are tickled at our steps. "Look at those black feet move."

"The audacity of them to climb,

don't they know, they are most beautiful when they dangle?"

I wonder, what they are more afraid of,

the boogeyman or the black man,

or are they still the same person?

I wonder, are they tired yet?

Are they not bothered by the blood on their hands?

Are they not worried about the bloodstains on their clothing?

So obsessed with the very thing they fear.

I wonder,

how many dead black bodies does it take to start a revolution?

What will they do when the spirit of Nat Turner is loosed

unhinged and released into fearless warriors who accept nothing but life-

too tired of playing on Ouija boards

just to say good morning to their fathers.

When the meal suddenly changes,

and the ground has to adjust its cravings-

Realign its appetite for beige appetizers

and fair skinned entrees...

Regurgitating and feasting

on its own systemic vomit.

I wonder will they be ready?

ATTACHED

Before you kiss him,
I apologize in advance for my scent.
I swallowed him whole, years ago
And he's never been able to wash me off.

NUMBER BROWN

Home.

A place where you can only be what you used to be.

That's why I don't visit much.

SINGING IN THE SHOWER

I heard her singing in the shower.

I heard her melodies collide with the water

and wondered how it felt.

It was the place she felt most comfortable.

It was her safety net, and I wondered how it felt.

Pondered how wonderful it must be to stand in a shower and sing in the rain.

Pondered how wonderful it must be to stand under the water and walk out clean.

Some people can bathe and take showers in a matter of minutes, for they are only washing away the day.

And then there are people like me, who never get a chance to sing in the rain.

Our notes never get a chance to collide with the water.

We are too busy scrubbing off the childhood rape,

And wiping away his scent;

Stuffing our ear canals with water trying to rinse out the sound of our mother's denial.

Steaming off his fingerprints,

Wishing to be scalded by the hot water… maybe then we could feel clean.

Praying that the pipes would spew boiling hot water

to burn off his cologne,

that often found itself draped around my mother's neck,

though it never choked her the way it choked me.

Wish it could burn my mind,

at least then it would fog up the windows of my memories, these are too vivid to keep.

There are scars on my head and lacerations on the nape.

I physically tried to cut the memories out!

And she sings in the shower.

Isn't she lucky?

BIG MAMA

Thick skin lathered in wisdom, thin layer of discernment.

hair of wool, silver follicles escaping her bronze scalp prove that her
thoughts are treasure.

Breasts of comfort, feed babies, feed generations,

hide currency and penny candy.

Sacs of family secrets, recipes, remedies.

Smell like peppermint and buttermilk.

She be looking for her branches. "Where dem babies et?"

Need to know they've been clothed,

Been fed, tummies and soul full.

"lemme hold that baby, you ain't holding him right"

Been holding our heads up since birth, trained our chins to be erect.

We don't look down unless we say grace.

Her feet heavy, walk the floors at night

House smell like prayers of repetition

Have always wanted the same thing.

"Lord, cover my children"

Know how to make poverty taste like prosperity.

Know how to dance, even when the song is sad.

Know how to love, even when it's hard.

Know how to make the wooden house with the patchy grass,

feel just like a home.

Remember the sting from her hot palms,

burning correction into my thighs like a branding iron.

We were hers- we did not belong to the world.

She know secrets, know God,

best friends with Jesus and ain't afraid to meet Him.

Thousands of moons done turned her pupils gray,

skin cracked, but her foundation still new.

She pass it off like germs, keep it going like gossip.

Dare not allow a day of her living to be in vain.

Coffin gone be full, because some things she'll never tell.

And when she leaves,

the world will be empty because some things

cannot be replaced.

REPROBATE

Washed me clean, just to go back.
I ain't good for nothing, except getting Holy water dirty.

LOW

Today, I didn't want to be black

Didn't want to be woke

Didn't want to be religious

Didn't want to be political

Didn't want to be woman,

Giver of life, or anything deep

Didn't want no titles or labels

Didn't want to fill no position, fulfil no promise

Just wanted to hide under my bed, become one with the floor.

Get as low as I physically and possibly could;

Just to match the way I feel.

EVEN SO

Carry my bible

Quote my scriptures

Cry out in my secret place

Fast and meditate

Speak in tongues

and still burn like the women, who do none of these things.

NUMBER WHITE

Punched the clock, like I wished it were my boss.

Her beige privilege is so tacky.

She is so interested in me.

Pushing my buttons, testing me out.

I am aware, but quiet.

She should fear the roaring silence that is approaching.

Even I am unsure of the damage it will cause.

Lemme get outta here...

GRIP

III.

NOT QUITE LIKE THEM

We are not our mothers' daughters, begging you men to stay

after you've spilled seed; Such reckless farmers, you are.

We do not leave the doors unlocked,

in hopes that you will return to help raise the children.

We do not watch the children wait for you. You are not coming.

We do not watch the children yearn for you.

You are too toxic for their system.

We do not force-feed you to them.

It only makes them cry, just as our mothers made us.

We do not call them by your name. No need to continue the curse.

We do not paint the house in your shade, build it in your structure.

No need to remind them of what rejected them.

No need to feed them to a house that has no taste for them.

We go where the love is fresh.

Where it is safe to yearn for fathers, who are good for their system,

easy on their stomach...soft on their heart.

We give the children a new name, and they walk differently.

Steps are a bit lighter without the weight of a curse.

Again, we are not our mothers' daughters...we are a different breed.

ILLEGAL EMBRACE

The night allowed us in, my skin to his skin.
His breath was the wind that spoke peace over my flesh.
Come in dear man and give all that you have left.
Interwoven with one another,
compelled to undress for his flesh to fit in my flesh.
We made love.
And he took me places I had yearned to go.
Hidden castles, forbidden passages, buried treasures and time capsules.
We made love.
Love that led to underground tunnels, acting as pathways to pleasure,
and stairways to euphoric islands.
We made love.
Chocolate kisses, silkened embraces and golden touches.
We made love.
Strawberry tongues over caramel mounds,
coated with passion and desire.
Wrestling in sheets too thin to contain
the ever so present dopamine in my brain,
Comparable to the rush of cocaine, and I am an addict.
Tussling in a bed too small to occupy my ebony high
as he reached and grabbed my ebony thigh.
We made love.
And love made us.
Heated winters and frozen springs, as I gushed and erupted,
and blew down the levee as a hurricane with no remorse.
We made love,
and love made us.
And before the sun could intimidate the moon,
He had returned home to his wife, asleep in their bedroom.
And I was left to my sheets, and my colorful metaphors
and they could not hold me.
I was alone…

5PM

I wanna go home. Blast my favorite song, let the pitch be my butler,

pull my feet out my shoes and let the notes massage my soles.

Let the bridge undress me.

Zipped up my full this morning.

Tummy tattooed from my girdle. It's time to be free.

I want my mounds to be reckless and fall where they may.

Get a whip of this room temp.

Inner thighs abolished from a spandex bondage.

Dents and knots, like misbehaving children fresh from punishment

finally get to come out and play

Breathe babies breathe

I want my shoulders and my back to wiggle,

carried the weight of the world- Let me put this Earth down.

Want my fingers to catch the beat, let the music know I'm grateful

Let God know, I'm soothed.

Want the coils in my hair to turn and twist like my hips,

want them to stretch and get comfortable

Corporate America been itching all day.

I want a glass of cool water, with 6 ice cubes

the day done got me hot.

Been baking in conformity.

Been cooking in restrictions.

And all I wanna do is go home and blast my favorite song,

and dj in the nude- and when I do,

I don't want nobody bothering me

REBOUND

He uses me.

I remind him of her, and a piece of me hopes I play her well.

THE AMERICAN DREAM

The alarms laugh boldly.

Laugh at our restlessness.

It is time to get up.

Rush to get ready. Rush to be stuck in traffic.

Rush to be on time,

to a job for which, we've overstayed our welcome.

Coffee brewing

while dreams of more, stale away in a canister nearby.

Swimming check to check, in society's ocean

with waves of inflation and shores of debt,

for which none of us have been equipped to swim-

but we all manage to barely stay afloat.

The 9-5 quickly becomes the next thirty years of life.

We live the same day, every day

becoming victims to routine.

It is the American Dream that no one ever realizes

is the most common nightmare.

THE TELLING KISS

His kiss, usually tastes like commitment. Like fidelity.

The texture of trust.

Usually taste like the peaks of my inner thighs.

Usually smell like the last six years that we've been together.

The lining of his mouth usually draw the shape of faithful,

shaded with loyalty, traced with promises.

His face masked beneath an epidermis of a familiar man,

who usually smells sure. Usually smells Locked.

But tonight, he smells unlocked. Opened.

And the stench, louder than a subwoofer in Houston, had me mixed up.

Ruptured the ear drum in my heart.

The smell, so loud my nose went deaf.

His kiss, usually tastes like commitment. Like fidelity.

The texture of trust.

Usually taste like the peaks of my inner thighs.

Usually smell like the last six years that we've been together.

Tonight, his kiss taste like foreign objects, like a third wheel;

His kiss taste like puss from an infection,

a wound so new that it has yet to even scab.

Tonight his kiss smells like infidelity, the texture of deceit.

The rotten taste of bodily fluids; those which do not belong to me.

Smells like a crime scene. Someone has stolen his love.

And it smells like love, fading.

Tastes like love becoming too comfortable.

Taste like love looking for love in other places.

And the only reason I recognize the taste,

is because I usually rinse it out of my own mouth

before I come home at night.

So now, in what should have been the calm before the storm,

is a shared space of mutual conviction.

And tonight, in the most twisted way we are finally on one accord.

Tonight, in the most perverse way, finally we are on the same page…

Just in two separate books.

BREAKFAST COGNAC

It was Monday morning, 9am.
James anxiously sat in the lobby. awaiting his interview.
His black was sure and certain, prompt and punctual.
His education was fresh, verified, he was no longer a statistic.
His income was pending and his experience was non-existent.
But he still smelled like confidence,
knew his value,
knew he was an asset,
knew this company could not pass him up.
"James, they are ready for you"
He walked into a room full of white privilege
scented with Starbucks and bagels.
They gestured, sang trivia in unison,
wanted to know why he thought he'd be good for the job.
James loosened the necktie that his grandfather gifted
him for graduation.
Grand-daddy cried tears of emancipation
looking at the cotton roped around James' neck and
thanked God it wasn't a noose, because grand-daddy still remembered.
James cleared his throat
and filled himself with conformity-watered himself down.
Could have been a Cognac, dark and strong
but instead, let his black sink to the bottom of the shot glass
while "I hope my black is white enough" rose to the top.
What used to be a black knight suddenly merged into a chameleon,
even mentioned something about golfing, though he'd never been.

At least he got the job though, right?

SELFISH SIMPLICITY

The boy child was coloring in a book, shading in a lion.
The girl child was rocking and bobbing, humming her favorite song.
The man was resting on the couch, still dressed from work.
I saw them, and had not a care in the world.

There were some people on the tv, arguing about politics and crime
upset about some white house shindig and gas prices
saying that the world was a horrible place to be.
And for the life of me,
I just couldn't relate.

PLAYGROUND

In 1982, before Sweety knew she was black

knew she was dark skinned, before she knew that her hair was nappy

before she knew that even though her scalp blows kisses of kinks,

everybody don't like suga.

Before she knew she was fat

before she realized that even if her heart was pure,

folk didn't feel like peeling through her ebony lipids to find out.

In 1982 before she knew her brother Isaac was gay,

knew he was different, got whooped more than the other children.

Before she knew she wasn't supposed to share her dolls with him.

Before she heard the tears drop from her father's face

every time he looked at Isaac.

Before she understood that those tears came from his own demons.

Before she ever heard someone call Isaac a faggot,

ever heard someone call her a nigger.

Before she ever felt a pressing comb or a perm,

Before Isaac ever had the church folk rebuke him and entice him,

pray and lay hands, then repent from laying hands.

Before either of them ever heard their mother's secret phone calls

about how much Isaac looked like Mr. Johnson from two blocks over.

Before they both were told to stay away from Uncle Harry

Sick from midnight cravings for young genitalia.

Before they were told they couldn't attend sleepovers-
They were pretty much happy kids.
I'm not sure why life fixes a plate of too much, too soon
and stuffs it down the throats of children,
rough swallows and bruised tonsils as the innocence fades.
I'm not sure why life won't just let the children play...

MISSES METAMORPHOSIS

Monday morning.

Awaken.

Greet 5:30.

Meditate in silence, while the sun prepares to shine.

Pressed my attire the night before.

Raisin Bread, with cream cheese.

Primp prime, arrive for work on time.

Pockets full of smiles, to be given at random

for I have achieved a space of contentment.

And then I met you.

Monday morning.

Overslept.

Hit the snooze button twice.

Missed the sun walk down the aisle.

Wanted to iron my clothes last night,

but they were soaked in tears.

No room for breakfast, from the heartache lodged in my throat.

Late for work.

Still on time for depression.

And it hurts to smile, for I didn't listen when they told me to run.

It was horrible to make your acquaintance.

NUMBER TEAL

I heard that there is a joy in being alone.
I'd like to find the liar who said that.

SHE HOTEL

She learned early on that inside of her,
was where men would crash into peace.
So she aspired to be nothing but cushion.

BREATH

IV.

BATTLE BATTER

Can we please argue in vanilla?
It is much harder to be angry when the words are sweet....
Much harder when the weapons rolling out of the mouth
taste and smell so good.

DRAPES & CANINES

I remember coming home too soon.

Seeing my father go up and down through the window.

The curtains were too thin to hide his indiscretions.

Too thin to hide the silhouettes of betrayal.

A mixture of sweat and disrespect; I can only imagine the smell,

though I truly don't remember the scent.

His body going up and down like a yoyo,

now a mirror of my mothers' emotions.

She was up, more so down.

Values, are easily lost in routes to wet vaginas.

Pussy make you forget boutcho family sometimes.

I remember her key not working.

remember how he weighed down on the door

weighed heavier on mama's heart.

Remember, being stuck in the night air on my own front porch,

until Miss Denise could grab her things.

We were immigrants, with no access to home.

Daddy let her escape and then he let us in,

wearing nothing but a brown robe and guilt.

Mama knew she married a dog,

found pieces of tics and fleas throughout the house.

Miss Denise left her bra.

TIIED

I am so tired of the stares. The random interviews about my hair
wanting to touch it as though it would make you cultured.
I am tired of the surprised faces, when I speak proper grammar
or when I do not yell, or when I leave my pajamas at home.
I am tired of my existence offending others' existence.
And I've been tired for a long time.
Tiied of feeding yo babies. Pink lips to brown breast
My nipples done dried up, can't feed my own child.
Tiied of you takin' my man, then mockin me fa bein alone.
Tiied of cleanin' up afta you, cleanin' up yo mess.
Tiied of buildin' this country up fa you,
While you tear us down.
Tiied. been tiied.
Tired. Been tired, for many moons.
Tired, on many realms.
Tired, in every time zone
Of you laying low and watching my black,
Taking notes on my black, condemning me for my black
And then appropriating my black.
I'm tiied of how you do my black.
But I am not one ounce weary or tiied of being black.
I can handle my black, love my black, wouldn't trade my black,
for no otha' shade…
Just tiied, is all.

NUMBER RED

My mouth is awful.

Hosting profanity and cavities and fleshly shafts.

Multiplying lies and underhanded compliments

Sticky tongue.

Angry tongue.

Untamable tongue.

I wonder, does God smell the filth when I pray?

CALL WAITING

My mama was on the phone with Aunt Pat.

Had the house smelling like gossip

smelling like sisterhood

smelling like the best audible you've ever heard!

Smelling like "shut that screen door, before you let them mosquitos in!"

Smelling like "hurry up and get out, you see I'm on the phone!"

Grown women, verifying, comparing notes, repeating the rumors,

but only to each other-

mama and Aunt Pat wasn't messy.

This conversation was good,

had me counting how many days it would be before I turned grown.

I couldn't wait to smack my lips, throw my shoulders

and use fake sign language.

Mama was acting like she needed to be excused during church.

Her index finger dancing stiffly in the kitchen,

bobbing her head yelling "Exactly! That's the same thing I said"

Aunt Pat must have said something so juicy,

mama couldn't catch the verbal liquids quick enough.

Mama's mouth broke open, said "SHUT UP!"

Commanded silence, but would have passed out if Aunt Pat quit talking

Traces of black-eyed & kidney things started falling out of the phone,

Aunt Pat was spilling the beans.

Oh they were cooking up a divine meal with the spillage.

I tried to get just an ounce of their talk,

but Mama wouldn't let me get a tablespoon.

Saw my shadow in the hallway, and said "who is that?!"

was waiting on an answer, like she wait in January for her w-2's

waiting on her cycle to come after a wild night in August

waiting on the dealership to run her credit,

so she can get that green monte carlo

even if her credit was bad.

I tilted my head in the room, hoping to see some more beans.

Mama pressed the phone against her chest,

like her titties were a mute button.

Told me through closed teeth, "Get outta grown folk's conversations!"

No need to go to school with a bruised lip, trying to prove a point,

I respectfully told her "yes mam".

They cackled

They laughed

They yelled

They were each other's secret keepers, best friends, shoulders to lean on,

"let me borrow $40 till Friday",

"Whatchu cook, cuz I'm hungry"

And I couldn't wait to get grown, just to find out

what all the talk was about.

WATERS

He would never. Has never

laid a hand on me, and would die before reacting violently.

But that day he came in, with her scent relaxed comfortably on his skin,

and her fragrance physically assaulted me.

It wrapped itself around my neck until my pulse began to slow dance.

Her smell boasted its weight into my home,

and corrupted the very foundation like a resentful tornado

angry from too few fatalities.

She was allowed to enter, but she didn't have my consent.

She was an invited intruder.

Never set foot in my living room, nor laid her body on my sheets

but she, in all of airborne glory,

still contaminated every aspect of this now silhouette of a home.

My heart debated on whether or not it would beat;

nearly stopped from the pain. Flooded waters escaped my eyes.

Soaked up the carpet that we laid down last spring.

Swallowed my kitchen, and I feared for my children,

for I knew the current could not love them.

The waters reached my thighs

my mothers' lamp floating on oceans

that were promised to be contained by fidelity.

Water at waist level, while our marriage license floated away.

Heard our vows gurgling as the levels continued to rise.

Wanted to interpret, but could not speak water.

Needed to know her name, but my lips imprisoned my tongue,

closed my throat like a crumbled up highway

and I could only envy the rubble.

The water rose to my belly, where our family expanded;

Where I housed 3 babies in water, and now my home was in labor.
Pushing life out.

What did she look like? How much was our family worth

and long has she been financing the cost with her divided thighs?

I wished I were a mermaid, then I could be easy in these waters.

What is her name!

Who is this woman that has beaten me without meeting me?

A mirror sailed through the hallway, caught a reflection of my husband-
a mere knot of tangled flesh, roped with lustful disregard.

His soul now tied to hers, while the threading from our unraveled.

I went from a woman, to a shoestring...Undone.

Untied from what I thought was triple knot marriage.

Someone found a loop.

I looked right through him, a shell of a groom with no words of
remorse- Just an empty stare, big enough to pack his belongings.

The water now above my chest, while memories began to sink

and sacred recollections began to seep beneath the front door.

He looked at me.

Wanted me to be okay, wanted the rivers from my eyes to stop flowing,

though he was perfectly fine being wet.

I saw my babies get caught in the cold waters, tears blended with waves
nostrils filled with inconsideration.
would have rather built sandcastles, but daddy preferred the sea.
It would be the last time that he and I exchanged such vital three words.
With anguish, he said "I love you",
with honesty, I said "I can't swim"

CALLOUS

Your love is so good,

I want to pinch myself to see if you're real,

But love has beat me so bad, I got no good skin left to pinch.

Funny thing is, you had good skin in the beginning

but kept pinching it, to make sure I was real too.

Love is so peculiar

AN ODE TO FREDRICK

Nights ain't so dark and winters ain't so cold, since he came

I had tears and issues. He had ears and tissues.

And he absorbed and listened to every pain that I could put into words.

When I wish to give up and stop dreaming, quit in the middle

his handprints forced against the small of my back,

refusing to watch me fail-He pushes me.

And it is the sweetest domestic abuse.

His mouth, a house of encouragement. Each panel, a soft word.

Each window, a verbal resuscitation.

He speaks life to every dead thing in me.

He endured the thick rotting smell of my dying heart.

Peeled the layers of my daddy issues.

Peeled the layers of self-hatred.

Peeled the layers of depression

and dared the generational curses to come closer.

Turned me into a good thing, like a family recipe.

A good thing, like a daddy who ain't allergic to fatherhood.

A good thing, like a baby being born to two people who love each other.

A real good thing, like seeds falling on fertile ground.

And I owe him so much.

Currency could never cover the charge.

I'd rather pay him in heartbeats and loyalty.

I feel blessed knowing, that since he touched me,

I am uncharted territories.

My body, foreign lands to foreign hands.

His is the only acceptable passport.

I pray for him.

Uterine prolapse, because I carry him-carried life for him.

Stretched the walls of my womb, for the lineage

and I am still unable to pay the debt.

His mother named him Fredrick, but I call him gratitude.

I keep finding more ways to tell God thank you

for loving me so much that He sent him.

I call him vision.

He saw beauty in all of my broken pieces.

I call him love, because well,

what else could he be?

NUMBER ORANGE

When my father dies, I believe I'll feel better.
It will then justify his absence.
It will finally align with my long dwelling truth-
that he's been dead for a while now.

TUESDAY

No matter what you do or say, my life won't stop for you.

If you leave now, or wait a few days

I still got these bills,

still got these kids,

still need to call mama at 4 to remind her to take her medicine,

still gotta go to work in the morning,

still gone drop you off in my prayer closet-

you too heavy for me anyhow,

and I'm still going out with the girls this weekend.

This break up is like a Tuesday;

It's happening, no matter what.

GOOD MORNING

Good Morning!

This is a new day dawning.

I hope you've obtained rest, for there is work to be done.

Boldly greet the sun, and capture what is yours.

Please dear Lord, cut the umbilical cord

to that dream

that vision

that goal

for birthing is nigh.

Contractions disguised as distractions have gone on long enough.

It is now time to push.

Rise from your angry bed, who becomes furious at the sight of you,

because your dreams are too big to contain.

It's too much weight on the bed frames.

Good Morning!

You are a soldier. Assume your position!

Be prepared for nothing less than war and opposition.

The enemy is approaching and he will find you.

He'll be dressed in the clothing of your friends,

The voice of doubters and the smell of nonbelievers.

He'll throw verbal ammunition, because you refuse to keep sleeping.

You gave in to this feeling in the pit of your stomach,

and could no longer stomach

the dormancy of sprouted inspiration or rotting motivation.

You were just about to bury in the dream cemetery,

but the Son, in the form of the sun,

boldly peeped through.

Eyelids squinting, legs stretching

and heart pumping gallons of fresh ideas,

all before your feet hit the floor.

Good Morning!

This is what you have been waiting for.

Go!

Run!

Jump!

Dive if need be!

This day is in your possession, you own every second.

Arise!

The Morning is here!

NUMBER GRAY

He picked up my pieces so good,
he made me glad that you broke me.

STEADY

Ooh girl look at him! Looking as good as a Friday!

Wonder what he like to do on the weekends?

Wonder can he work with my weak ends?

Life done pressed me down, love done shook me apart

but I am running over with optimism!

I can't miss out on a good thing, still talking bout the bad things.

Naw naw naw!

I still need me some love, need me some phone calls,

need me some hugging and kissing

need me some eye contact

need me some date night, late night,

just gone and spend the night so we don't miss nothing.

I ain't worried bout them slick Jacks, Dirty Hanks or nobody else!

They hurt me but that's quite alright.

I still ain't gone be afraid to love.

It feels too good, when it's real...to just let it be.

Now let me go and offer him a drink of my presence,

see what his sips be like.

LOOSED

V.

THE GRIZZLY & THE RAIN

When my knees part and the rain falls
the grizzly keeps quiet, is peaceful
and the home is still.
Even though the dirty dishes are taller than the children
and the laundry has mildewed.
Twice cycled-forgot I started.
And the stove may be bare, like the family is fasting
but the grizzly will not come out,
will not stomp, beat his chest, grumble nor shake the air
because the fallen rain keeps him at peace.
But when the drought comes,
even if the dishes are new, and the floor is golden,
and the stove is covered with heart soothing recipes,
plates and frills,
that grizzly comes out
stomping and roaring, fisting and kicking
and beating against his chest
until my knees part and the rain comes down again.
It is the only weather that soothes him.

2ND FLOOR GAMBLING

Thursday afternoon. Been on my feet. Been on this clock.

I catch the elevator so I can finally be free.

Kayden, stitched in beige,

stares with eyes that have never felt oppression.

A long stare, bold stare, a dissecting stare.

Our eyes meet, I give my corporate greeting,

to which opens her prodding, and the picking begins.

"Is that your real hair?" she asks. "It's just sooo pretty!"

"Can I touch it?" she says.

What the hell is taking the elevator so long?!

Maybe, this isn't even an elevator.

Maybe this is an exam room, and my hair is scheduled for a pap smear.

Or maybe this is a dental office

and my hair has some type of cavity or gingivitis

and Dr. Kayden needs to go in and take a look!?

Her back handed compliment left a foul odor in the tiny space,

And my hair was such an acronym- a fallacy.

A black woman, with beautiful hair-how in the world, could that be?

She actually waited on my response

as though it were change from a transaction.

Like it was owed to her.

But my braided culture..coconut oil rituals were not up for picking apart,

but I was up for a trade.

I leaned in gently and told her

"of course, but only if I can touch your privilege"

The elevator doors finally parted, and I am not sure which felt better,

the fresh wind or the look of her flushed cherried cheeks.

Either way, we never made the trade.

FLOWERS

When you die, they will put on their mourning attire.

heavy hearted and distraught.

Bring you flowers that you cannot smell

flowers that you cannot see

flowers that you cannot touch.

They will wail, knock their bodies against your new wooden home

and become crushed when no one answers.

They will stain your coffin with sorrow

and wish you were still here.

We always assume we have more time.

Bypass apologies, sleep good on mattresses stuffed with turmoil,

lips sewn shut with pride, heart layered with arrogance

and time, with its swift legs, is still running out.

She wanted to say "I love you",

wanted her to know that she was sorry for their stupid fight,

wanted her to accept her apology,

but dead people can't accept apologies.

can't hear your wailing

can't smell flowers

can't see flowers

can't touch flowers.

HEAD

You are golden.

You are necessary.

And this house stands upon your shoulders.

Your voice straightens the spine of these children.

Your steps shake these walls.

Your hands are the biggest in the home.

Your clothes smell like work-always smell like work.

Your boots come off where they may.

Inside of me is your home- use your key often.

You are the man of this house,

And God is pleased.

THIS BREEZE

Sweet like peaches.

Sweet like Sunday mornings, like 70 degrees in August,

this breeze don't owe me nothing.

I could feel the wind, stroking the back of my neck,

like it knew I was tense.

Two bills in each palm, rent is still due, and time is so stuck in her ways,

that she waits for no man.

I asked her twice to slow down, so I could catch up with myself.

I lost my mind four times, as though it were lubed with oil

and my hands had no fingers, for which to hold

but this breeze don't owe me nothing.

It blew the dust passed my lashes.

I closed my eyes for two seconds and was reminded

that the dark ain't always bad.

And silence ain't always given,

sometimes you have to steal away to hear it.

He pricked my heart on purpose, and laughed at the blood. I paid the
metal thieves to come and rob me of his seed, a rotten fruit I refused to
bear. I was in bondage for so long, that my liberty was uncomfortable,
but this breeze don't owe me nothing.

The cool current parted my mane, like my mama used to do, before I
understood her struggle with words. Always saying she was fine, but
always meaning, she was broken. Always saying "God is good", always
meaning "why hast thou forsaken me?" I can only imagine how hard it
must have been to be the head and neck of a home, built on shaky
ground, always trying to walk with her balance in tow, but this breeze
don't owe me nothing.

At the family reunion, I see more generational curses than family members. Pink elephants in Big Mama's living room, bones stacked in each closet, and no one discusses what really happened to Alexandria, but this breeze don't owe me nothing.

My boss called and said that the company is downsizing, but my children are upsizing, my rent is upsizing, and my expenses are upsizing and this is the worst time to get laid off! My tears, now afraid to fall, because I just lost my health insurance, treaded lightly down my face, and were carried away with the wind.

My children are running rampant, and my husband's belly is vacant, and my sense of self, drowned years ago, in the waters of life. I was not prepared to swim in such crowded waters, where so many would cling to my hips, bearing more than just babies. Cling to my nipples for sweet necessary nectar. Cling to my arms, to make sure I swam close, just in case God troubled the waters, but this breeze don't owe me nothing.

It reminds me that I am still here. I forgot to feel. I forgot to dream. This breeze was like a fresh wind, injected into stale lungs of a withering body, one breath away from being a corpse. I realize that I was just going through the motions of life; too distracted to live.

This breeze reminds me that I have time. Reminds me that the Maker is still breathing. Reminds me to breathe ..for me. Live.. for me..

Dear God, this breeze don't owe me nothing.

BOUND
THE BREAK –UP POEM

He was the biggest heartbreak of them all, my chest is still recuperating.

Stings a little with every heartbeat, and I never could stop loving him.

He took me away from myself, turned me into a revolving door.

He came in and out of my life as he pleased,

kinda reminded me of my father,

had me dizzy from all the back and forth.

But I am done! I could never let him back in.

He served me pain on a hot dish and I was too desperate to fast.

He stabbed me

and I loved him so hard,

I tricked myself into thinking that the blade was made from sugar

thought I'd get a sweetheart.

Just the other day, I found an old shirt of his in the closet.

Much like an onion, had me weeping-tears of freedom.

I hope life is feeding him hot stool!

I wish he was dehydrated, I would pack up this pain

put it in a plastic bag and force it through his IV.

I hope someone hurts him, the way he hurt me.

I hope every time his heart beats,

it stings his chest. burns his chest. scars his ch-

knock, knock, knock

I'll have to finish this poem later,

he's here to pick me up.

PRELUDE

My coiled up mane is thick and big and purposed

Roots grow upward, tall, obvious.

Make me a gardener,

if I don't tend to it, it won't grow

Make me a spectacle,

if folks didn't stare, it wouldn't be right.

I pic my hair out as big as I can, like I'm searching for gold.

Make sure my daughter know it's okay to be curly,

so she don't curl up into a corner, uncomfortable being herself.

We pay homage to the ship-riders with our braids and beads.

Sometimes, I twist it,

other times

it twist the folk around me.

Mama said "when you gonna get a perm?"

Boyfriend volunteered to buy weave

work said it was offensive.

For someone else, this is the prelude to conformity.

For someone else.

FAT

This guy had the nerve to call me a fat whore.

I saw the words hop scotch off his tongue,

I saw the color of the air change, could smell his insecurities

smelled like a bowel movement, still moving, and I still didn't shrink.

Felt no conviction during my second plate of collards,

asked for the hot sauce and another piece of bread.

Your words ain't never fed me.

Get full off of pinto beans and jiffy.

These legs, these fat legs, done parted for secret peepshows

parted to braid cornrows; add beads and accessories,

hold babies in the sanctuary, while my spirit get fed.

These arms, these fat jiggly arms,

tattooed with grease poppings

make beds, prepare tables, family ain't never went hungry

wash clothes, sprinkle in seasonings just like my mama taught me.

Pass the paprika, chop up some onions, stir it real good,

make today taste like a Sunday

These titties, full brown titties, make the young girls stare—

can't wait to grow up and have.

They are the comfort when my husband is hurting,

they quiet the babies, soothe that colic

hold my money and my keys when I leave my purse in the trunk.

This neck and chin, this double chin

keep me humble, make it hard for me to look down on folks

This body is lightening, everybody won't survive the storm.

This body is prize, can't get it unless you win.

This body is weekend, can't wait for it to get here.

This body is tradition.

Knots and curves like my mama and Aunt Neecee.

Got arms like Big Mama,

God zipped me up and called it a family reunion.

This body is wrapped in thick skin,

hold in all this glory, hold in all this blessing.

hold in all this magnificence.

And there is no way, you can make me hate it.

MARITAL TRANSITION

I am mourning the loss of myself.

Bereaved for many moons, though I don't remember dying.

Mattress empty, sheets cold.

Why sleep, if I no longer dream?

Someone went away with me.

Someone is enjoying the dead that I've become.

I used to breathe on purpose, now it is an obligation.

They need me.

I became another woman.

Draped in breast milk, and finger jewelry.

Single women envy me, and secretly, the feeling is mutual.

What happened to me?

I cook and feed them, though inside I have no hungry.

There are days I go looking for me

wondering is there a lost and found for selves

And has anyone turned my self in?

I rub pages of my old diary against my new skin,

but the stories never feel familiar.

I try to wear my old garments, but they never fit appropriately.

Try to go out and live, but the freedom feels selfish.

I have been this woman for too long.

Does anyone remember what I did with me?

BANKING

When banking, you can only withdraw, that which you've deposited.

You simply cannot get out, what you do not put in.

Some days, people try to get out of me, that which they've not put in.

There are moments, when I give what I've not been given

and it leaves me in the negative-insufficient-overdrafted

with nothing left for myself,

except an empty account of where something, for me, used to be.

These are the times I wish I were a bank.

SUMMER '96

At thirteen, Reese has yet to bleed.

She is worried that the shift won't come

constantly seeking the black cherry serum that all the girls chit and chat
about.

"What is taking so long?" Ain't my body a body, ain't this vessel a girl?"

Wanna know why when she jump in the ocean, sharks don't come.

"Ain't I good enough to eat?"

She wears this crown of confusion like headbands and barrettes.

Her mother prepared a period kit ten months ago

it is now older than her little brother

just sitting on the shelf, collecting dust.

Sometimes, she think since she made in the image of Christ

maybe she need to be hung, crucified, maybe then, the blood will shed.
Some days she sit on the toilet for hours

wondering why the water ain't pink

why her body won't pass the clotted evidence

that her body is a body, her vessel is a girl.

Wanna know what robber is lurking on her insides,

holding the blood hostage.

She saw her mother's face light up, when she told her she was cramping

dimmed to dark, when they realized it was just the milkshake.

Her mother is worried, prays daily for blood, like a hungry vampire.

Told God, she'd sacrifice anything for her daughter's period to come.

Her mother's hair began to thin,

the frail strands, gently decorated the framing of her face.

Her beautiful and full crown, now vanishing.

She changed hairstyles, wore hats to church

sometimes, she'd let the evening air massage her scalp while she sat on the porch.

So many people perplexed by her perfect health, yet fading hair

Weeks later Reese woke up in a pool of her own blood.

She screamed for her mother, afraid but relieved.

"My body is a body, this vessel is a girl!"

Her mother, now completely bald, cleaned her

gave her the period kit,

made her some tea and a pallet in the den.

Her mother returned to the blood soaked sheets

embraced them and cried rivers of gratitude.

A bald woman on her knees, thanking God for blood and head wraps.

ABDUCTED

Today, while I was out
I saw some "Missing" flyers, with my face on it.
I quickly snatched each one down and balled them up.
I placed the trash in my purse and went about my day.
I have been lost in your love for a while now.
I pray they never find me
I like it here, with you.

AN ODE TO FREDRICK
PART II

I can take every blessing, on a delayed schedule

as long as the wait is with you.

You are bible pages, in flesh form.

Proof that God has been here.

You are a face and body, prostrate.

Took instructions on what to do with me.

You are intercession, before the request.

Wrote the petition, and God rewarded.

You love me, in a spiritual place.

In a place I can't physically touch.

You love me, in a place that makes my broken pieces want to rebuild
themselves.

I am not the Walls of Jericho. I am loved.

And you love me, through my soul, just the way I am.

You love me so much

you never changed a thing a single thing about me,

except my last name.

ACKNOWLEDGMENTS

This collection could not have been created, had it not been for those around me. They shared pieces of themselves and walked in their raw truths, for me to see. This is how I learned that imperfection, in the end, can swell into a great thing. I appreciate them for allowing me to soak and sponge all that was before me; my life is a complete reflection of their transparency. My hope is that you allow your own pieces and those around you to form something great. I pray that you live out loud and on purpose and never ever resent your pieces.

ABOUT THE AUTHOR

 Ejspeaks is widely known for her comedic storytelling, although she is much more than a comedian. With this book, she sheds light on another aspect of conveying a story. Determined not to be boxed in, she has allowed the world to see just how multi-faceted she is. When asked where she gets inspiration, she quickly gives a full list of amazing craftswomen, including her own mother, Maya Angelou, Jill Scott and a plethora of others. Even as a child, Ej was known to be funny, charismatic and colorful. Her mother never took that away from her; she was always allowed to be free and lively. And now as a woman, she has perfected her storytelling and is quite ready to share so much more with the world. This is only the beginning.

To learn more about Ejspeaks, go to: www.ejspeaks.com

For booking inquiries, email: bookejspeaks@yahoo.com